Management Extra

FACILITATOR'S GUIDE

Management Extra

FACILITATOR'S GUIDE

Routledge
Taylor & Francis Group

LONDON AND NEW YORK

eLEARN

First published by Butterworth-Heinemann

First published 2005

© 2005 Elearn Limited

All rights reserved

This edition published 2011 by Routledge
2 Park Square, Milton Park, Abingdon, Oxon OX14 4RN
711 Third Avenue, New York, NY 10017, USA

Routledge is an imprint of the Taylor & Francis Group, an informa business

British Library Cataloguing in Publication Data
A catalogue record for this book is available from the British Library

Library of Congress Cataloguing in Publication Data
A catalogue record for this book is available from the Library of Congress

ISBN 0 7506 6829 6

Contents

Preface

In recent years there has been a shift in thinking about the role of a manager, much of it articulated in the concept of transformational leadership. Ideas have also been changing about how best to help managers learn. Managers need relevant skills to help them be flexible and manage their demanding lives.

Management Extra is a series of books designed for self-paced learning. Each combines core concepts in a topic area with a rich mix of activities. A companion website provides resources that complement the books including diagnostics, workshop materials and assessments.

This guide is written for management development practitioners. It describes the Management Extra series and how you can use it for formal and informal management development activity including:

◆ Skills, attitude and competency based programmes

◆ Qualification based programmes including vocational and academic management programmes.

1 Changing directions in management development

'New business forces demand a different approach to the development of employees. Capable and committed people have become the critical source of competitive advantage. Emphasis must be shifted from training as a series of top-down interventions to a focus on individual learning.'

Focus on the learner,
Chartered Institute of Personnel and Development (2003)

Until not so very long ago, management development meant going on a course. Now there are a plethora of approaches to choose from.

20 ways to learn	
360-degree feedback	Qualification based programmes
Psychometrics	Internet searches
Performance review	Communities of practice
Coaching	Action learning
Mentoring	Development centres
Buddy systems	Outdoor learning
Secondments and job swaps	Learning from others
Books and learning resources	Acting up
Workshops	Project working
Elearning	Reflection on experience

Table 1.1 *20 ways to learn*

In particular, there has been a surge of interest in more personal forms of learning support including elearning, mentoring, coaching, 360 degree feedback, action learning sets and secondments – all of which are situated in the workplace. There are various reasons:

◆ The development of personal leadership skills is a high priority that is not easily achieved through classroom training.

◆ The competitive pressure to respond rapidly to new business conditions and opportunities means that training needs to be responsive and able to be implemented in a faster moving environment.

◆ The onus is now on managers to take responsibility for their personal development and this is fuelling a demand for learning that can be applied instantly to workplace issues.

♦ Managers need learning that is flexible and fits with their demanding role.

♦ Research indicates that managers would prefer to learn in the workplace than the classroom (Logenecker,2002).

Despite their popularity, informal learning processes pose issues for employers. They are more labour intensive to support and are difficult to evaluate. They presuppose the workplace to be a supportive learning environment and individuals to have the motivation and skills in self-reflection to learn from it.

Focusing on the learner

The challenge then for management development practitioners is how to exploit this diversity of learning opportunity in a way that meets the needs of both the organisation and the individual. Pressing questions include:

♦ How can development be fitted into the busy lives of managers?

♦ How should management development take on board research about how managers want to learn?

♦ Which is best: a holistic approach to management development or an approach in which relevant training is accessed as and when required?

♦ How can managers access learning to solve problems at work?

♦ Can development meet the needs of the individual and the organisation?

The transition from a trainer-led approach to one that focuses on learner choice and flexibility is challenging and demanding. But the end destination is compelling – the potential of an organisation composed of self-confident individuals with an active desire and capacity for learning is a striking vision for most employers.

The role of Management Extra

Management Extra is a series of books designed to support a self-directed approach to management learning. The books offer a wide range of benefits:

♦ They offer flexibility to the learner, empowering them to choose, what, when and where to learn.

♦ They provide a challenging, but accessible body of management knowledge.

♦ Learning is continuously applied to the workplace through activities.

♦ The high quality format raises the image of a training programme and helps to impress on the participants that they really do matter.

◆ They comprehensively cover a wide range of management and leadership topics and can be used as knowledge inputs for most qualification based management programmes (see cross matching schemes on www.managementextra.com).

◆ The books are a cost and time-efficient approach to development, reducing the time required in the classroom.

About this book

This book is about the Management Extra series and how to use it to develop learning programmes that increase flexibility and choice for the learner. It is divided into five sections:

◆ **The Management Extra series** highlighting how the books and website are designed to support learning and facilitation.

◆ **Making learning flexible** exploring the design principles for successful flexible learning programmes.

◆ **Management Extra in practice** providing examples that show Management Extra books and resources can be used to support a variety of management development programmes.

◆ **Customising Management Extra** providing advice on how to extend and tailoring the content to achieve a better fit.

◆ **The Management Extra resources** describing the content of the books and the website.

2 The Management Extra series

Management Extra is designed to help learners put ideas into practice. Each book combines thought-provoking ideas, examples and theories about the key management concepts of our time with activities to help learners see how the concepts work in practice. If you include time to complete activities, each book provides about 30 hours of learning material.

Titles include:

- Managing Yourself
- Positive Working Relationships
- Leading Teams
- Development for High Performance
- Managing for Results
- Financial Management
- Quality and Operations Management

- Change Management
- Business Environment
- Project Management
- Information and Knowledge Management
- Reputation Management
- Recruitment and Selection

Key features of the books

The books are written to support learning:

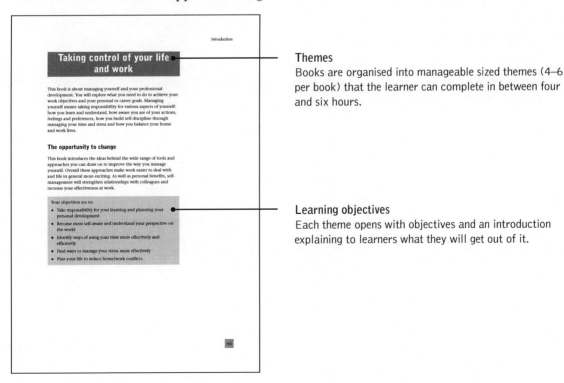

Themes
Books are organised into manageable sized themes (4–6 per book) that the learner can complete in between four and six hours.

Learning objectives
Each theme opens with objectives and an introduction explaining to learners what they will get out of it.

Figure 2.1 *Features of the Management Extra books*

Engaging and accessible

The books address topical issues of relevance to most managers and are written using straightforward language that assumes no prior knowledge.

Examples

Examples and case studies that show how the theories and concepts work in practice.

Attractive layout

Designed as an interactive workbook with space for notes and activity responses.

Activities with formative feedback

Each book contains a rich mix of activities that help learners develop their learning, apply it to live work issues and keep track of their progress. Typical activity formats are:

– Know yourself type assessments

– Reflective activities

– Right way – wrong way case studies

– Application activities to bring in information from the workplace

Feedback helps the learner to assess their answers and to compare their thinking with those of the author.

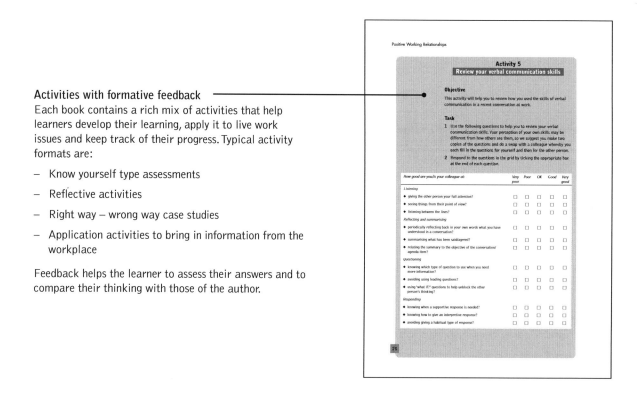

Positive Working Relationships

◆ Recap

Explore models of effective interpersonal communication

◆ Communication involves an exchange of meaning, achieved through the processes of coding, transmission, decoding and feedback.

◆ Transactional analysis describes three ego states (behaviour patterns) that each of us can adopt when interacting with others: Parent, Adult and Child. The ideal transaction is Adult to Adult.

Identify factors influencing organisational communication

◆ Organisational culture has an impact on communication, influencing the extent to which organisations codify and diffuse information.

◆ Organisational trends, including new media, team and project working and delayering, mean that communication is now more direct, informal and immediate.

Identify the main barriers to effective communication

◆ The main barriers include physical surroundings, language and jargon, and cultural diversity.

◆ Barriers can be overcome by paying attention to the context of communication, selecting the right medium and trying to see things the way the receiver does.

Skills for improving verbal communication

◆ Listening, reflecting, summarising, questioning, responding and feedback are essential skills for verbal communication.

◆ When your body language or tone of voice is inconsistent with the words you are using, your overall message is diminished and can even be contradicted.

▶▶ More @

Adair, J. (1997) *Effective communication: the most important management tool of all*, Pan
This book explores basic communication skills and then goes further to look at presentations, visual aids, interviews, appraisals, giving and receiving criticism, and communication between departments

Recap
A summary concludes each theme recapping the key issues against each of the objectives.

More@
Books and website links are recommended for further reading on each theme.

References

References

Adair, J. (1997) *Effective communication: the most important management tool of all*, Pan

Adair, J. (1983) *Effective Leadership*, Gower

Alberti, R. E. and Emmons, M. L. (1978) *Your Perfect Right*, Impact.

Back, K. and Back, K. (1999) *Assertiveness at Work*, McGraw-Hill.

Barker, A. (1997) *How to Hold Better Meetings*, Kogan Page

Barker, A. (2000) *Improve Your Communication Skills*, Kogan Page.

Barlow, J. et al. (2002) 1st edition, *Smart Videoconferencing: New Habits for Virtual Meetings*, Berrett-Koehler Publishers Inc.

Berne, E. (1968) *Games People Play*, Penguin

Boisot, M. (1987) *Information in Organisations: The Manager as Anthropologist*, Fontana

Caunt, J. (2000) *Organise Yourself*, Kogan Page

Covey, S. R. (1992) *The Seven Habits of Highly Effective People*, Simon & Schuster

Dickson, A. (2000) *Women at Work*, Kogan Page

Fayol, H. (1916) *General and Industrial Administration*, Dunod

Fisher, R., Ury, W. and Patton, B. (1991) *Getting to Yes*, Century

Fleming, I. (1997) 4th edition, *The Time Management Pocketbook*, Management Pocketbooks Ltd

Gillen, T. (1992) *Assertiveness for Managers*, Gower

Goleman, D. (2000) *Working With Emotional Intelligence*, Bantam

Guirdham, M. (1995) *Interpersonal Skills at Work*, Prentice Hall

Handy, C. (1993) *Understanding Organisations*, Penguin Business

Harris, T. (1995) *I'm OK – You're OK*, Arrow

Hawkins, P. and Shohet, R. (1998) *Supervision in the Helping Professions*, Open University Press

Heller, R. (1998) *Communicate Clearly*, Dorling Kindersel

The Herald (2001) 'Raising confident children', Part 3, 26 May Supplement

Hindle, T. (1998) *Managing Meetings*, Dorling Kindersely

Holland, S. and Ward, C. (1990) *Assertiveness: A Practical Approach*, Winslow

Hunt, J. (1982) *Managing People in Organisations*, McGraw-Hill

Full references
Full references are provided for further advanced study, assignment or project work at the end of each book.

ManagementExtra.com

ManagementExtra.com is a companion website to the series. It offers management development practitioners a range of stimulating and relevant resources that can be integrated into learning programmes that use the Management Extra books.

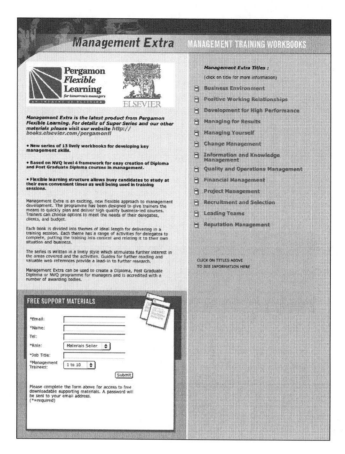

Figure 2.1 *ManagementExtra.com*

Site registration is free and provides access to:

♦ a download version of this guide

♦ sample themes from the Management Extra books

♦ cross-matching schemes against national qualifications and standards.

Subscription to the site provides access to current and relevant programmes resources that have been developed to support Management Extra including:

♦ Workshop programmes including facilitator guides, activity handouts presentation aids for each of the books.

♦ Sample assignments.

♦ Programme and project briefing resources.

♦ Further reading articles.

For information on how to subscribe to website or to access the free resources, visit www.managementextra.com

3 Making learning flexible

At a strategic level, there might be consensus on the need to make learning flexible, but at a tactical level it is more challenging. This section explores the issues and provides guidance on how to create flexible programmes of learning.

Getting the balance right

What exactly are you empowering learners to do? This question forms the start point for our design process; there are two aspects to consider:

♦ **Who decides the objectives of learning – the individual or the organisation?**
 Learners will be more engaged and committed if they can decide for themselves what to learn and apply. The extent to which this is possible is contingent on the situation. Health and safety is an obvious example where the organisation has to prescribe the objectives. Compliance based training is another. Most management development programmes though – even academic programmes with a recognised curriculum – can be designed to offer learners scope to realise their personal and workplace performance goals.

♦ **Who decides the means for learning – the individual or the organisation?**
 Choosing how to learn is a decision that traditionally has been taken by the organisation and all too often means a 'one size fits all' training course.

Standard taught courses with pre-determined goals and learning methods typically offer little choice to the learner. They are rigid in approach and are often disconnected from the live issues that managers face in the workplace. That said, the training course is still an extremely effective vehicle for developing managers, but it needs to be re-positioned alongside other learning approaches as part of an overall blend that recognises diversity of individual learning need and preference.

The move from the periphery to the mainstream of workplace learning support tools like coaching, 360-degree feedback and self-paced learning resources greatly increases the potential to help managers link learning more closely with their work and to offer them flexibility to choose how, what, where and when they learn.

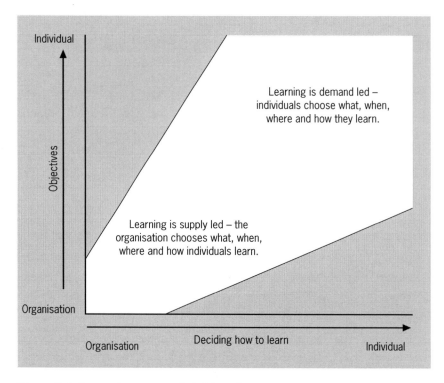

Figure 3.1 *Demand versus supply led learning*

A transparent and structured learning process

While there has been an enthusiastic embracing of more flexible forms of learning by organisations, learners may not be ready for the form of self-directedness demanded by flexible learning; nor necessarily are their employers equipped to support workplace learning that is flexibly delivered.

An essential difference between flexible learning and classroom-based training lies in the transparency of the learning process. It is the individual learner not the facilitator who steers the learning and it is crucial that the programme provides them with the support and information they need to manage their learning.

A framework for learning

Brokers of self-managed learning advocate that organisations need to develop a strong architecture for management development and create within it a capability for individuals to manage their personal learning.

> *'It is about being responsible to learners by providing appropriate support (structure) so that they can really take charge of and be responsible for their own development.'*

Cunningham, 2000

The framework in Figure 3.2 identifies four critical stages in a learning programme and highlights for each the types of support that a learner might need.

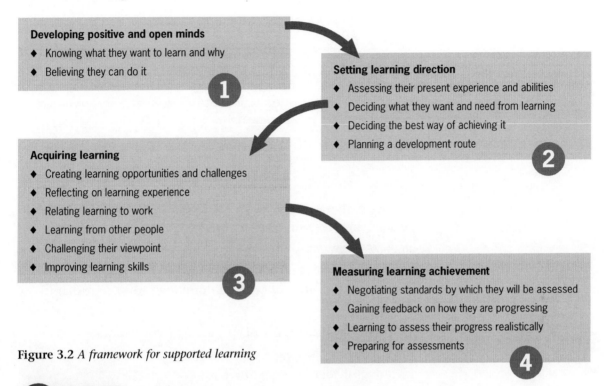

Developing positive and open minds
- ◆ Knowing what they want to learn and why
- ◆ Believing they can do it

1

Setting learning direction
- ◆ Assessing their present experience and abilities
- ◆ Deciding what they want and need from learning
- ◆ Deciding the best way of achieving it
- ◆ Planning a development route

2

Acquiring learning
- ◆ Creating learning opportunities and challenges
- ◆ Reflecting on learning experience
- ◆ Relating learning to work
- ◆ Learning from other people
- ◆ Challenging their viewpoint
- ◆ Improving learning skills

3

Measuring learning achievement
- ◆ Negotiating standards by which they will be assessed
- ◆ Gaining feedback on how they are progressing
- ◆ Learning to assess their progress realistically
- ◆ Preparing for assessments

4

Figure 3.2 *A framework for supported learning*

1 2 3 4 Developing positive and open minds

A positive and open mind is one that is receptive to new ideas and information. The key question that you are seeking to satisfy at this stage is *'Why should I join this programme?'*

How people feel about learning is very important to the success of the learning experience. People's attitude to learning is shaped by a combination of the extent to which they believe the training is relevant to them, their past experiences of training, and their own levels of self-confidence.

Here are some ways you can help learners develop a positive and open mindset.

- ◆ Consider how you can make the learning feel fun and exciting or have interest to the learner before they start.

- ◆ Encourage learners to explore how they can achieve personal and workplace goals through the programme.

- ◆ Run launch events and emphasise what's in it for the learner; be clear about why a busy person invest their time in this programme.

- ◆ Provide colourful and stimulating handbooks or welcome packs that provide road maps for the programme, identify contact points, resources and sources of information.

- ◆ Discuss barriers to learning and ask learners to identify how they might overcome them.

♦ Find ways to raise learner expectations and help them visualise success.

♦ Engage line managers so that they can encourage learners.

♦ Raise curiosity by posing intriguing questions.

1 **2** 3 4 Planning learning direction

Planning learning direction is about supporting learners to reflect on their skills and experience, helping them to identify performance gaps and to plan for learning. It is is about answering '*What do I want to learn?*' and '*How and when should I learn it?*'

Here are some techniques to consider:

♦ Provide activities, self-assessment diagnostics or psychometrics to help learners recognise strengths and limitations.

♦ Encourage learners to develop self-awareness by seeking feedback from others. Use feedback activities like 360-degree appraisal, development centres or collate information from performance reviews.

♦ Help learners make sense of conflicting information.

♦ Offer coaching support to encourage setting of personal and meaningful goals for the programme.

♦ Provide development planning tools to help the learner map the programme to their personal and workplace goals and to set targets.

♦ Create opportunities for early wins.

1 2 **3** 4 Acquiring learning

People learn in different ways. We need to embrace this fact and create learning that is truly learner centred and appeals to the range of ways that people learn:

♦ Use a blend of learning approaches to suit the context and training need.

♦ Create flexibility so that people can select what to learn.

♦ Provide coaching support to develop learning skills, in particular skills in self-reflection and the skills to integrate learning from diverse sources.

♦ Encourage learners to tackle live managerial problems and issues during the learning.

♦ Encourage the linking of theory to practice through action learning, work projects, assignments or coaching.

♦ Create opportunities to learn from personal experience and from the experience of others.

♦ Build in opportunities and provide support for critical reflection.

◆ Offer feedback and challenge, most people have deeply ingrained patterns of behaviour and providing opportunity for reflection may not be enough to encourage personal change.

1 2 3 **4** Measuring learning achievement

Assessment is often associated with qualification programmes, but assessing learning and the impact of learning is particularly important for self-managed learners. Assessment needs to provide direction and motivate the learner through the learning process, providing a sense of achievement as they confirm newly developed skills and knowledge and apply them to real work issues at each stage.

There are three types of assessment to consider:

Diagnostic assessment
◆ Assessment **before** learning
◆ Informal
◆ Identifies Knowledge and skills gap
◆ Helps learner set direction and plan for learning

Formative Assessment
◆ Assessment **for** learning
◆ Informal
◆ Provides feedback
◆ Helps learner measure progress and adapt learning plan

Summative assessment
◆ Assessment **of** learning
◆ Formal
◆ Assesses what was learnt
◆ Makes a judgement on learner achievement and provides learner with results and feedback

Figure 3.3 *Programme assessment*

In practice the different functions of assessment are not clear-cut but properly overlap and integrate. Consider how to:

◆ Measure whether learners have become better managers, not just whether they have better management knowledge.

◆ Integrate a mix of formative activities within the learning process that help learners develop and assess their own learning. Management Extras provides a wide range of formative activities.

◆ Encourage regular review of achievement against learning goals and critical reflection on learning.

◆ Situate assessment in the workplace so that learners can link their learning with their work.

◆ Provide flexibility within the assessment process for learners to tackle live work issues.

◆ Consider assessment options beyond written assignments or computer-based tests; for example, performance feedback, achievement of goals, project presentations, presentation of workplace evidence.

◆ Provide group and individual support activities to help learners understand the assessment process and to develop the skills to be successful.

4 Management Extra in practice

In this section, we provide examples that show how Management Extra can be used alongside other development approaches to create learning programmes that offer flexibility and choice to the learner. The examples have been derived from actual programme structures to illustrate how Management Extra is used in practice.

The examples explore the following aspects of learning:

◆ Skills and knowledge learning, which combines self-paced learning with facilitator support to develop specific knowledge and skills.

◆ Leadership development, which blends performance support tools with learning resources, coaching and action learning to develop leadership capability and increase corporate business knowledge.

◆ Accredited learning, which combines a programme of self-paced learning with workshops and workplace assignments to achieve fixed assessment outcomes and a qualification. Examples are provided for both academic and vocational qualifications.

◆ Attitude-driven learning, which mixes various events and delivery media to develop specific behaviours and change attitudes.

Example 1 – Skills and knowledge learning

This example shows how Management Extra can be used to introduce flexibility into a short project management course. This is a popular application for flexible learning that works best when people are learning at the content or at the application level. It enables workshop contact time to be focused on skills development and applying learning in context rather than on the knowledge-related learning which is achieved through the learning resources.

The benefits extend beyond creating a time-efficient blend. This format aims to foster longer-term commitment to project management principles than a taught workshop might achieve, by involving substantial practical elements with constructive feedback and good follow-up after the course is completed.

The programme offers learners self-paced learning from Project Management, a skills development workshop and coaching support to apply their learning to a workplace project.

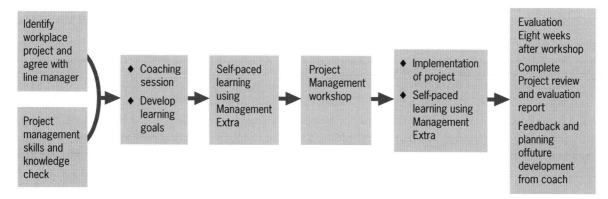

Figure 4.1 *Using Management Extra for short courses*

How it works

Developing a positive mindset	◆ Learners receive the *Project Management* book and a Welcome Pack describing the course, the benefits that accrue from it and how to prepare for their first coaching session.
	◆ As part of their preparation, learners are asked to develop an idea for a 'live' project to work on during the course. Activity 3 of the Management Extra book provides guidance.
Setting direction	◆ A skills and knowledge check helps learners assess their present ability.
	◆ With the support of a coach, learners set improvement goals and explore how they can use the course to achieve these.
Acquiring learning	◆ Learners use concepts and activities from the first three themes of *Project Management* to improve the definition of their project and to create a project plan.
	◆ Weekly contact from the coach helps motivate learners to prepare for the workshop.
	◆ During a one-day workshop, learners work in small groups to share key learning from the project definition and planning stages and to provide feedback to peers. Skills development activities focus on project implementation and in particular project leadership.
	◆ Learners use the final two themes from *Project Management* to support implementation of their project.
Measuring learning achievement	◆ Learners are asked to assess the strengths and weaknesses of their project and to submit an evaluation report to their coach. A date for the evaluation is agreed at the workshop, nominally six weeks.

Resources to support this programme are available from ManagementExtra.com.

Example 2 – Leadership development

This programme, which is designed to develop management talent and increase corporate knowledge, is needs based and uses the workplace to develop leadership and job competencies. It is the most learner-centric of the examples in this section, creating the potential for individual managers to develop entirely personalised programmes of learning and assessment. Commitment and support for learning from line managers and senior managers are both critical components for this programme.

Individual learning needs are met through a combination of coaching, learning resources, learning events and action learning based around live workplace issues. Management Extra provides the core learning resource and is supplemented by strategic documents from the organisation including business plans, annual reports, market research and so on to form a knowledge hub for learners.

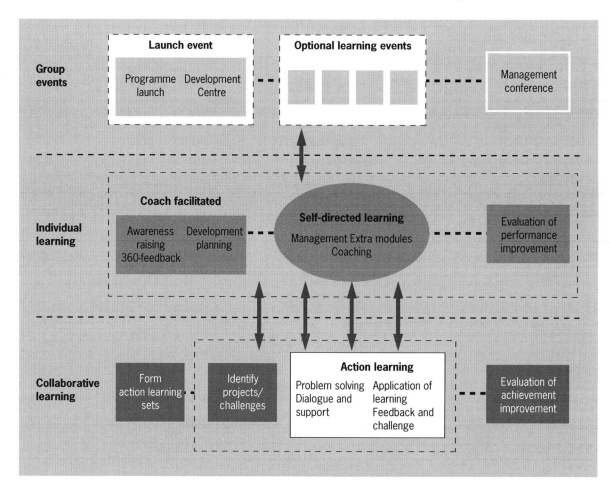

Figure 4.2 *Using Management Extra for leadership development*

How it works

Developing a positive mindset	◆ Individuals attend a launch event that explains the learning process, emphasises the benefits and provides opportunity for learners to meet and form a support network. A launch pack offers guidance on the learning process.
Setting direction	◆ The emphasis is on developing self-awareness and planning a learning route.
	◆ Learners work with their coach to reflect on their skills and behaviour using feedback from an observed development centre and a 360-degree feedback activity against a framework of leadership capabilities.
	◆ In consultation with their line manager, learners plan strategic opportunities and challenges in the workplace to help develop their capability. A development plan captures goals, learning events and targets achievement levels.
Acquiring learning	◆ Learners work in action learning sets (4-5 people) to provide peer support and coaching around workplace issues. The set facilitator directs learners to relevant resources, including Management Extra.
	◆ Optional learning events including skills development workshops and topical presentations from internal and external people is available to all learners. Learners collaborate to identify learning events and themes.
	◆ Regular coaching sessions encourage participants to critically reflect on progress against their development plan and to apply new learning.
Measuring learning achievement	◆ The main measure of achievement is against the goals set out in the development plan.
	◆ Learners present an assessment of their learning and on-the-job performance at a management conference, six months after the start of the programme. The aim is to bring together ideas, encourage knowledge sharing and to raise awareness of future learning options.

Resources to support this programme are available from ManagementExtra.com.

Example 3 – Accredited learning – Certificate in Management

Providers of qualification-based programmes are recognising the benefits of a modular structure and flexible delivery to their learners. The example below uses Management Extra as the primary means of learning for a Certificate in Management programme.

The programme offers the flexibility of self-paced learning within a tightly scheduled group learning plan which includes start and end dates for modules and assignment submission deadlines. Sustaining momentum for the duration of a qualification based programme can be challenging, and the group schedule is an important element in encouraging learners to make continuous progress.

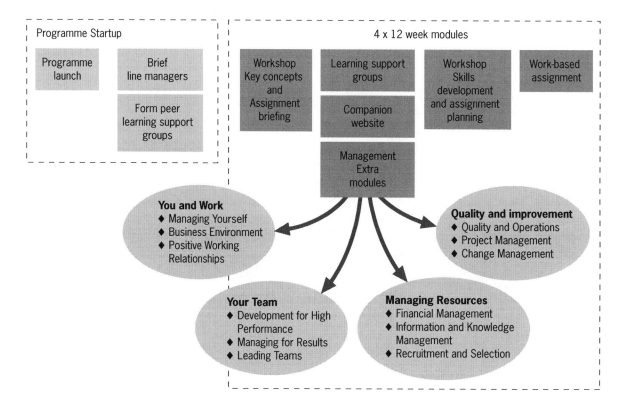

Figure 4.3 *Using Management Extra for a Certificate in Management*

How it works

Developing a positive mindset	◆ Most learners joining a qualification programme will be motivated by the prospect of the qualification. Partly their mindset will be won.
	◆ Despite a positive desire to join the programme, learners are often concerned about their ability to succeed; they might not have learnt for some time or they might be concerned about finding time. A vital element of induction is to help learners visualise and plan for success.
	◆ The learning support group is an important support network. Forming the groups and helping them to gel is also imperative.
Setting direction	◆ Workplace assignments are provided as flexible frameworks within which learners can create a focus for their own learning for each module.
Acquiring learning	◆ Management Extra resources are matched against the syllabus and grouped into module clusters. The books that are required for each module are distributed at the key concepts workshop at the start of each module.
	◆ Workshops focus on capturing and contextualising key points from the learning, on skills development and on assignment planning.
	◆ Management Extra activities are for self-study and also as the basis of group activities in workshops. This helps learners to access the books.
	◆ Assignments encourage consolidation and further development of learning using live workplace issues.
	◆ A learning portal provides supporting articles from management journals and useful websites.
Measuring learning achievement	◆ The assignments play an important part in enabling learners to measure achievement and plan for improvement. Constructive feedback is provided in writing but also discussed with learners.
	◆ Support for assignment work plays an important part of both module workshops. Initially this focuses on helping learners to apply the assignment framework to their own workplace issues and on providing an environment in which they can test their thinking with peers.

Resources to support this programme are available from ManagementExtra.com.

Example 4 – Accredited programme – S/NVQ in Management

This vocational qualification offers learners a programme of on-the-job development activities with coaching and self-directed learning. The programme encourages a learning cycle of development planning, knowledge acquisition, practice and reflection. Each learner follows a personalised programme of development created from the management standards.

Figure 4.4 *Using Management Extra for a S/NVQ in management*

How it works

Developing a positive mindset	◆ A briefing workshop and welcome pack explain the programme.
Setting direction	◆ An interactive workshop of diagnostic tools and planning activities helps learners to create individual development paths against the standards.
	◆ Learners are coached in a process to create workplace development activities based on the standards. Management Extra activities support this.
	◆ Consultation with line managers forms a crucial part of developing feasible workplace activities.
	◆ Learners consolidate the diagnostic and planning work into a development plan.
Acquiring learning	◆ Management Extra resources are matched against the management standards.
	◆ Professional development activities created by the learners with the support of their Development Advisor form the main focus for learning.
	◆ Facilitated action learning sets provide a supportive environment for learners to share learning practice.
	◆ 1:1 coaching sessions each month with the development adviser focus on critical reflection and planning.
Measuring learning achievement	◆ Formative assessment is provided on an ongoing basis by the Development Adviser.
	◆ Final assessment involves presentation of a portfolio of evidence.

Resources to support this programme are available from ManagementExtra.com.

These include a cross match of Management Extra against the management standards.

Example 5 – Attitude driven learning

The desired outcome for this programme is to change the behaviour of first line managers to increase their focus on developing their teams. Collaborative workshops and action learning sets are an important focus for the programme providing a risk-free environment for practising new skills and sharing tacit knowledge. Management Extra resources are used to challenge people's mindsets by exposing learners to new ideas, concepts and best practice. The line manager plays a key role in supporting and providing feedback to learners.

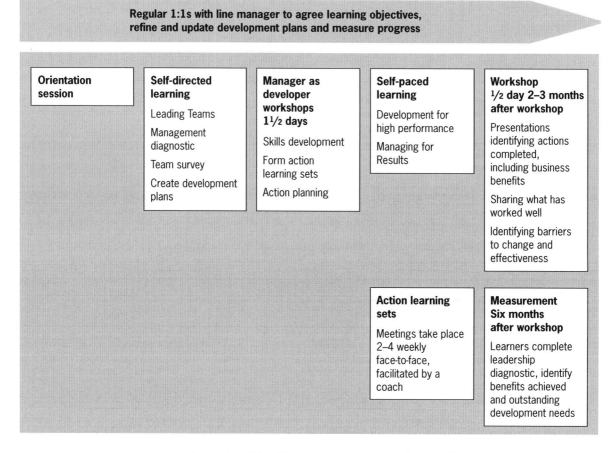

Figure 4.5 *Using Management Extra for behaviour change*

How it works

Developing a positive mindset	◆ At an orientation session learners receive an induction pack describing the course. Motivational resources including guru videos are used to raise enthusiasm.
Setting direction	◆ Feedback from diagnostics and a Team Motivation and Performance survey is used by participants and line managers to identify development direction.
	◆ A development and action plan captures how they will develop their own leadership skills and the capabilities of their team over a 3 month period.
Acquiring learning	◆ *Leading Teams* sets the context for the workshop.
	◆ The role of manager as developer of people is the focus for the workshop . The workshop provides a risk-free environnment for role playing and trying out new behaviours.
	◆ Facilitated action learning sets provide an opportunity for exploration of issues and reflection on practice as learners implement their development plans.
	◆ Additional Management Extra resources are used to challenge and develop participant mindsets.
Measuring learning achievement	◆ Learners present the outcomes of their work at a workshop, sharing what has worked and the barriers they face in change.
	◆ Six months after the start of the programme, learners repeat the diagnostics.

Resources to support this programme are available from ManagementExtra.com.

Finding the right blend

The examples all seek to optimise flexibility and choice for learners by providing a mix of learning experiences and delivery channels. Blended learning is now quite commonplace in learning design but it varies quite considerably in its execution.

The most powerful blended learning takes place when the components are designed to reinforce and cross-reference each other within an overarching and cohesive framework. Cohesion is achieved, not only through good design of learning resources, but also by incorporating collaboration and workplace learning which take the learner beyond the boundaries of the learning programme and into real issues that they face in the workplace.

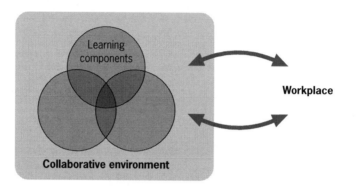

Figure 4.6 *Blending learning (adapted from Content and Context in elearning, Epic plc)*

So how should you choose the right blend of learning channels? While there is no formula for optimising the blend, some organisations have developed semiformal methodologies to support decision making about what methods to use and when to use them.

The following model which is adapted from IDC's Blended Learning and Business Change study (2003) proposes four criteria to consider:

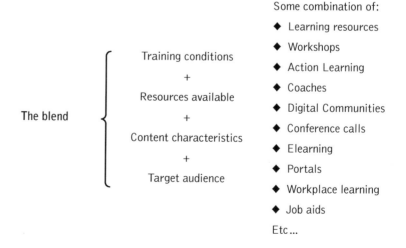

- **Conditions** in which an initiative is undertaken.
  Is it urgent to complete the training?
  Will results be reported externally?

- **Resources** available for a particular training need.
  Do we have the resources to cope?
  Do we have the development expertise?
  What is our budget?
  Is the blend scalable?
  Is the blend sustainable?

- **Target audience**.
  Do learners have access to physical classrooms?
  Do they speak the same language?
  How much time off the job can we support?
  Are they in the same time zone?
  Does the blend fit the culture of the organisation?

- **Characteristics of the content**.
  How valuable is the subject matter to the organization?
  Is the content informational, procedural, behavioral or conceptual?
  Which learning approaches are most effective for delivering this type of content?

Resources to support this process are available from ManagementExtra.com

Support for implementation

You can also obtain help to develop and deliver a blended approach from the authors of this Facilitation Guide:

Elearn	Contact:	Tony Horsfield
Gables House	Office:	0870 142 5697
29 Gateforth Lane	Direct:	01757 228882
Hambleton	Mobile:	07770 350 857
Selby	Fax:	01757 228823
YO8 9 HP	tony.horsfield@elearn.co.uk	
	www.elearn.co.uk	

Alternatively contact one of the following who are able to provide training services in support of the Management Extra series

Acorn Learning Solutions		
Somerton House	Contact:	Sarah John
Hazell Drive	Tel:	01633 663000
Newport	Fax:	01633 810400
South Wales	enquiries@acornlearning.co.uk	
NP10 8FY	acornlearning.co.uk	

Access Training
Ferintosh Business Park
DINGWALL
Ross-shire
IV15 9TE

Contact: George Grandison
Tel: 01349 865777
Fax: 01349 865865
george@accesstraining.demon.co.uk

Amaranth Consulting Ltd
PO Box 5277
Milton-Keynes
MK7 6BS

Contact: Jane Burns
Tel: 01908 671500
Mob: 07714 607115
jane@amaranth-consulting.co.uk
www.amaranth-consulting.co.uk

Crownship Development Ltd
Charlton House Mews
Bridge Street
BRIGG
North Lincolnshire
DN20 8NQ

Contact: Helle Smith
Tel: 01652 658151
Fax: 01652 658221
helle@crowndev.freeserve.co.uk
www.crownship.com

CTC
South Glebe Farm
Old Bawtry Road
Finningley
Doncaster DN9 3BU

Contact: Karen Trem
Tel: 01302 773277
Fax: 01302 772757
Mobile: 07811 328529
ctckaren@aol.com
www.ctc4business.co.uk

Ellerton Training Services
125 Grange Loan
EDINBURGH
EH9 2HB

Contact: Judith Warren
Tel/fax: 0131 667 5570
enquiries@ellertontraining.co.uk
www.ellertontraining.co.uk

Genesis Training
Alston House
White Cross
LANCASTER
LA1 4XQ

Contact: John Davies
Tel: 01524 843800
Fax: 01524 843806
info@genesistraining.co.uk
www.genesistraining.co.uk

GLC Management Solutions
7 Hillside Park
Bangor
Co. Down
N. IRELAND
BT19 6TU

Contact: Michael Crothers
Tel: 02891 455415
ilmireland@aol.com

The Learning Approach
Tower House
Fishergate
York
YO10 4UA

Contact: John Dyson/Kate Williams
Tel: 01904 567 313
Fax: 01904 567 336
info@thelearningapproach.com
www.thelearningapproach.com

Management Services (Midlands)

Calver House	Contact: Ken Ellis, June Hawkins
30 Marston Crescent	Tel: 0116 277 6330
Countesthorpe	Fax: 0116 278 0500
LEICESTER	info@m-s-m.co.uk
LE8 5PY	www.m-s-m.co.uk

Open Learning Centre International

24 King Street	Contact: Max Faulkner
CARMARTHEN	Tel: 01267 235268
SA31 1BS	Fax: 01267 238179
	maxfaulkner@olcinternational.com
	www.olcinternational.com

Vector Training Ltd

14 Clifford Street	Contact: Brin Bendon
York	Tel: 01904 621199
North Yorkshire	Fax: 01904 658845
YO1 9RD	enquiries@vectortraining.co.uk
	www.vectortraining.co.uk

5 Customising Management Extra

There are three main options for selecting learning resources to support a programme:

◆ Use off-the-shelf learning resources like Management Extra

◆ Plan and develop custom made resources

◆ Tailor and extend learning resources

Generally speaking, it is more cost efficient to buy or adapt proven resources than it is to create your own, but it does depend on how close the match is between your requirements and the package in the first instance. Table 5.1 highlights issues to consider.

Audience	◆ Who are the resources written for?
	◆ How similar is the target audience to your own?
Objectives	◆ How closely do the learning objectives match those of your own learners?
Coverage	◆ Are there areas of the text where you require more or less breadth or depth?
	◆ Does the text address topical issues in a 'up to date' way?
Relevance	◆ How relevant are the examples and activities to your learners?
	◆ Will the materials help our learners tackle current issues?
	◆ Are there other activities and examples that might be more helpful or relevant?
Pitch	◆ Are the resources pitched at the right level for your learners e.g writing style, vocabulary, sentence length.

Table 5.1 *Evaluating learning resources*

In most instances the match does not have to be perfect. A set of good core learning materials can be adapted to improve their relevance and coverage. For example, you might want to fill in gaps, provide more depth, offer contrasting viewpoints or provide local examples and activities. Here are five strategies to consider.

1. Add additional resources to create a knowledge bank

There are plenty of resources, which although not designed for learning, do an excellent job of getting the message across and provide very credible resources within a bank. Possible sources include:

◆ Websites. Links to management websites that provide information to support Management Extra is provided as an appendix to this book

◆ Journal articles

◆ Newspaper articles

- Company intranets and newsletters
- Policy documents and company handbooks
- Textbooks

2. Develop new resources

Creating new resources to add to the core package is another way to make the package more relevant and meaningful to your learners. Examples include:

- Locally relevant activities with feedback
- Case studies with organisation or sector relevance
- Organisation specific examples

3. Develop an Application Guide

An Application Guide or Study Guide advises learners how best to use the resources in context. It acts as a 'wrap around' helping to bind resources that are diverse in origin and format into a coherent and accessible whole for the learner. Depending on the context, an application guide might offer:

- Study guidance
- Learning objectives
- A road map through the resources and the programme
- Editorial to introduce resources
- Summaries of key learning points
- Advice on how to select and use resources
- Learning support tools like development plans and diagnostics
- Assignments for discussion with tutors or colleagues

4. Provide a learning portal

Learning portals present the learner with access to learning resources and information on demand. A learning portal could be used in conjunction with Management Extra to:

- Provide searchable access to further reading for each book
- Provide weblinks to other websites
- Offer scope for collaborative discussions
- Provide programme guidance
- Offer editorial and programme news
- Offer learning in other formats, in particular elearning and video

5. Tailor the resources

There might be occasions when you feel that additional resources are not the answer and you would prefer to tailor the Management Extra book itself. The two most common forms of customisation are:

◆ **Badging** which involves changing the physical appearance, for example the logo, cover style and print colours, to match an organisation's style and image.

◆ **Tailoring** which involves editing the content to achieve a better fit with the needs of a particular organisation, industry sector or training programme. This might include:

    – adding examples that have greater resonance with the target learners

    – tailoring the activities to support transfer to specific work environments

    – adding or removing some of the content within a book

    – re-arranging content between books so that they can be used more easily to support a particular course structure.

For more information on tailoring the Management Extra series contact:

Elearn
Gables House
29 Gateforth Lane
Hambleton
Selby
YO8 9 HP

Contact: Tony Horsfield
Office: 0870 142 5697
Direct: 01757 228882
Mobile: 07770 350 857
Fax: 01757 228823
tony.horsfield@elearn.co.uk
www.elearn.co.uk

6 The Management Extra books

This section describes each of the books that make up the Management Extra series. Current titles in the series are:

- Business Environment
- Change Management
- Development for High Performance
- Financial Management
- Information and Knowledge Management
- Managing for Results
- Reputation Management
- Managing Yourself
- Project Management
- Quality and Operations Management
- Recruitment and Selection
- Leading Teams
- Positive Working Relationships

Now available from Routledge

Business Environment

Business Environment looks at the major factors that influence an organisation's strategy. It equips learners with a portfolio of tools including PESTLE, portfolio analysis, capability audits, SWOT and stakeholder analysis to analyse the internal and external environment within which their organisation operates and challenges them to develop their understanding of their organisation's strategic direction.

Objectives

◆ To explore the nature of your organisation.

◆ To assess the impact of internal factors such as culture and structure on organisations.

◆ To conduct an internal environment analysis.

◆ To identify stakeholders and their impact on the business.

◆ To evaluate trends in the external environment that will affect organisations in the future.

◆ To explore your organisation's position in the marketplace.

◆ To use analytical techniques to uncover the opportunities and threats to your business.

Themes

The organisation in context

The organisational landscape

The key players

The macro environment

SWOT analysis

Change Management

This book explores change from the perspective of the organisation and from the individual manager. It considers how change affects organisations; how they respond to changes in the business environment, influence that environment and use change processes to gain competitive advantage. It explores the role of the change agent, and introduces tools and techniques for planning, launching and managing change programmes successfully. It describes the impact of change on individuals and emphasises the role of the manager in supporting individuals through the change process.

Objectives

◆ To understand your role in the change process and why change is necessary.

◆ To investigate external and internal forces for change.

◆ To explore how to develop and implement a change strategy, including launch strategies, management styles and targeting change.

◆ To use your knowledge of individual reactions to change to help you adapt your behaviour and achieve successful change.

◆ To adapt your approaches to cultural change.

◆ To explore the dynamics of organisational change and how they can be harnessed for success.

Themes

Why change?

The conditions for change

A framework for change

Individual and organisational change

Techniques for sustainable change

Development for High Performance

A key feature of the role of managers is to develop the people who make up their team. This book explains the development process and contextualises it against the overall aims, strategies and business plans of the organisation. It explores the role of the line manager in creating development opportunities and provides examples to show how managers can use coaching, mentoring, delegation and performance management to help their team develop skills and learn to work together effectively.

Objectives

♦ To identify how employee development is linked to organisational performance.

♦ To develop employees by leading, coaching, mentoring and delegating.

♦ To identify opportunities for people development when faced with organisational changes.

♦ To explore the competency framework and use it to highlight individual and team development needs.

♦ To apply the key steps within a performance management process.

♦ To evaluate the effectiveness of training and development activities.

Themes

Development for improved performance

Leading and coaching

Mentoring and delegating

Change and performance

Evaluating performance

Financial Management

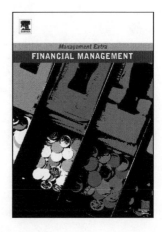

To gain competitive advantage all parts of an organisation must be able to talk to one another. It follows then that all managers must be, in some sense, financial managers who are able to speak the common language of finance. This book aims to provide learners with the necessary understanding to input into the financial management of their organisation.

Objectives

◆ To be able to contribute more effectively to the financial planning process in your organisation.

◆ To investigate the relationship between costing and pricing of products.

◆ To learn to prepare capital investment proposals.

◆ To use the main financial statements and key financial ratios to evaluate an organisation's performance.

◆ To identify the main sources of funding for an organisation.

Themes

Key financial statements

Preparing and monitoring budgets

Pricing for profitability

Reviewing financial performance

External reporting

Information and Knowledge Management

Individuals and organisations rely on their ability to select and process information, both to make sense of their local environment and to try to understand the bigger picture. This book approaches information management from two key perspectives:

♦ The skills of the individuals manager to source, manage and communicate information

♦ The organisational processes and systems for managing information and knowledge.

Objectives

♦ To identify sources of information relevant to your needs inside and outside of your organisation.

♦ To evaluate and improve the quality of your information sources.

♦ To learn how to manage information overload.

♦ To describe key principles for communicating effectively in writing.

♦ To identify the principles behind information system design and management.

♦ To explain the features of knowledge management.

Themes

Information, data and decision making

Evaluating information

Communicating information

Information systems

Knowledge management

Managing for Results

Managing for results focuses on how to get the best out of people and celebrate the diversity of perspectives and experience that people bring to your organisation. The book explores motivation and how peoples' needs affect the satisfaction that they get from their work. Practical activities encourage learners to consider a number of strategies for increasing the motivation and effectiveness of their team.

The book also considers how dissatisfaction impacts on performance and assesses the role of the grievance and disciplinary processes in managing performance.

Objectives

◆ To contribute more effectively to the overall goals and objectives of your unit and the organisation.

◆ To develop an understanding of how individuals and teams harness motivation to achieve results.

◆ To identify how individual expectations affect performance.

◆ To explore the nature of the rewards that individuals expect and link them to the results that are expected of them.

◆ To explore new ways of balancing the varying needs of individuals and the team when managing for results.

Themes

Specify the results

Motivation theory

Motivation to achieve results

Grievance and disciplinary procedures

A balancing act

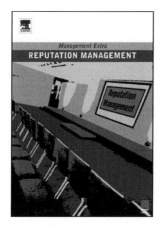

Reputation Management

This book provides a clear insight into the meanings that people attach to popular notions such as reputation, image, brand, public relations (PR) and corporate governance. It explains how organisations use reputation and image to create competitive advantage and how to manage situations where the corporate reputation is at risk. It also explores the role that the manager plays in building and managing the business reputation and image both inside and outside the organisation.

Objectives

- ◆ To determine the features that characterise the reputation of your organisation and the trade-offs that have been made to create an image that matches the corporate and business context.

- ◆ To assess the effectiveness of your organisation in creating and maintaining an appropriate image at corporate and business levels.

- ◆ To identify what is being done and what needs to be done to maintain effective brand images for both the organisation and the products and services that the enterprise depends on for growth and survival.

- ◆ To evaluate the value of techniques used in managing internal and external public relations.

- ◆ To assess how effective your organisation is at providing corporate governance and dealing with crisis situations where reputations may be at risk.

Themes

Image and reputation

Creating a corporate image

Managing brand image

Managing the internal image

Managing the external image

Managing Yourself

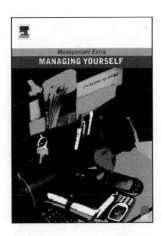

This book is about the skills of personal effectiveness and professional development. Learners are introduced to a wide range of tools and approaches that will enable them to realise their personal and work performance goals by improving the way in which they manage themselves. It highlights how managing yourself means taking responsibility for various aspects of yourself: how you learn and understand, how aware you are of your actions, feelings and preferences, how you build self discipline through managing your time and stress and how you balance your home and work lives.

Objectives

◆ To take responsibility for your learning and planning your personal development.

◆ To become more self-aware and understand your perspective on the world.

◆ To identify ways of using your time more effectively and efficiently.

◆ To find ways to manage your stress more effectively.

◆ To plan your life to reduce home/work conflicts.

Themes

Learning and reflection

Personal development and self-awareness

Exploring perceptions and diversity

Time management

Stress and life balance

Project Management

This book focuses on the activities involved in initiating, planning, implementing and completing a project successfully. As well as covering the tools and techniques of project management, it also pays attention to the soft issues involved – how to manage the people side of project management.

Objectives

◆ To explore what differentiates a project from other types of work and identify the essential stages in the project lifecycle.

◆ To define the vision, objectives and scope of a project with the project sponsors and key stakeholders.

◆ To identify the key elements of a project plan and practice network analysis techniques for project planning.

◆ To learn how to identify and manage potential risks in relation to the project.

◆ To find out what is involved in leading and monitoring a project effectively.

◆ To explore how to bring a project to closure, evaluate its success and capture learning points for the future.

Themes

What is project management?

Project initiation and definition

Project planning

Putting the plan into action

Project completion

Quality and Operations Management

This book considers the associated concepts of quality and operations and places customers at the heart of a quality business operation. It explains how organisations that are focused on delivering quality products and services continuously improve the design, planning and control of their operational processes so that they meet the developing needs of their customer.

Objectives

◆ To develop your understanding of quality as an organisational, team and customer concept.

◆ To explore and practice the application of quality tools and techniques to improve the quality of products, services and processes.

◆ To evaluate how you can plan and control quality in the processes you manage.

◆ To assess health, safety and the environment as quality issues.

Themes

The language of quality

Improvement

Quality in operations planning and control

Techniques for planning and control

Quality in health, safety and the environment

Recruitment and Selection

The red-hot competition for talented employees is still news. Employers everywhere recognise that they must evolve better recruitment, selection and retention strategies if they are to compete effectively with their rivals for the best people. This book discusses current practices in recruitment and selection and offers advice on how to take an approach that is strategically focused, effective, fair and based on best practice.

Objectives

♦ To determine the essential stages of the recruitment and selection process and the manager's role within it.

♦ To consider how to take account of equality and diversity issues including legislation and related codes of practice.

♦ To assess alternative approaches to external recruitment for addressing shortfalls in the pool of skills, knowledge, and experience.

♦ To profile a job role and develop information that describes the vacancy in fair, clear and accurate terms.

♦ To evaluate methods for attracting people from a wide pool of talent.

♦ To explore methods for selecting the candidate who is likely to perform most effectively.

♦ To develop a process for ensuring a positive start for a new employee.

Themes

Essentials of recruitment and selection

Profiling the role

Recruitment strategies

The selection process

Keeping new recruits

Leading Teams

Building and leading a successful team is one of the most valuable and rewarding management activities. This book explores why team working has become such a prevalent force in the global workplace and looks at the many different types of teams that now exist. It explores contemporary thinking on leadership, particularly situational leadership, action-centred leadership and ethical leadership and provides practical techniques to build teams and develop their performance.

Objectives

- ◆ To appreciate the pivotal role of teams in the workplace and the characteristics that differentiate high performing teams.

- ◆ To analyse your own leadership style and plan to develop your leadership skills.

- ◆ To explore ways in which you can build a high performing team.

- ◆ To plan to improve team working using the techniques of empowerment, team decision-making and team learning.

Themes

The shape of teams

Approaches to leadership

Leadership in practice

Team building

Strengthening the team

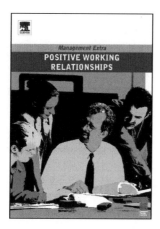

Positive Working Relationships

This book explores the skills of communication and assertive behaviour and how they enable openness and honesty to be brought into a relationship. It looks at how to develop better working relationships by applying these skills in three specific areas: negotiations, meetings and conflict management.

Objectives

♦ To become a more effective communicator.

♦ To master your ability to think and behave assertively in difficult situations.

♦ To develop your skills for leading and participating in meetings.

♦ To find out how to negotiate win-win solutions.

♦ To improve your ability to manage conflicts of interest and disagreements.

Themes

Communicating to connect

Behaving assertively

Making meetings productive

Negotiating win-win solutions

Recognising and managing conflict

References

Chartered Institute of Personnel and Development (2003), *Focus on the learner*, www.cipd.co.uk/NR/rdonlyres/6EF2BB45-6C9F-4744-8611-B856D2833C23/0/2837focuslearne03.pdf

Chartered Institute of Personnel and Development (2004).
Reflections – new directions in training and development

www.cipd.co.uk/NR/rdonlyres/3D57B6FA-81C6-41BB-8A21-D5717600A43E/0/2958reflctnstrndstraindevt.pdf

Bennett, B. and Dawes, G., edited by Cunningham I., (2000)
Self Managed Learning in Action, Gower

Cunningham, I. (1999), *The Wisdom of Strategic Learning*, Gower

Epic plc, (2003) *Content and Context in elearning*, www.epic.co.uk

Appendix – Useful weblinks

The section offers useful weblinks to support learning from the ManagementExtra books.

Working Relationships

Personal development skills including communication, problem solving, time management
www.mindtools.com

The Consortium for Research on Emotional Intelligence in Organisations
www.eiconsortium.org/index.html

Recruitment and Selection

The Chartered Institute of Personnel and Development offer excellent resources on recruitment and selection, workforce development and resourcing
www.cipd.co.uk

The Equal Opportunities Commission
www.eoc.org.uk

Leading Teams

Classical Leadership Models
www.infed.org/leadership/traditional_leadership.htm

Leader to Leader Institute – an excellent source of articles and opinion
www.pfdf.org/leaderbooks/l2l/index.html

Provides access to the 2005 management standards
www.management-standards.org

Belbin's team roles
www.belbin.com

Reputation Management

Corporate Reputation Institute at Manchester Business School
www.mbs.ac.uk/research/centres-projects/corporate-reputation/index.htm

Useful resources for managing PR agencies
www.prca.org.uk/sites/prca.nsf/homepages/homepage.

American Marketing Association website providing extensive marketing resources
www.marketingpower.com.

Another useful marketing portal
www.knowthis.com

Quality and Operations

Excellent toolkits providing practical advice from the Dti on business topics including quality, flexible working, diversity and communications
www.dti.gov.uk/bestpractice/people/flexible-working.htm

European Foundation for Quality Management
www.efqm.org

Institution of Operations Management
http://iomnet.org.uk/index.htm

Health & safety law
www.open.gov.uk/hse

Project Management

The Association for Project Management offering access to the Project Management Body of Knowledge
www.apm.org.uk/copyright/next.htm

Online library of free papers and articles. Particularly good for operations, IT and finance.
www.bettermanagement.com

Information and Knowledge Management

An excellent portal for exloring knowledge management
www.kmresource.com/exp.htm

Financial Management

Online learning resources in business, particularly finance and economics.
www.bized.ac.uk/learn/learn.htm

For annual reports
http://annualreports.money.msn.co.uk

Business Environment

Excellent overview of strategic analysis and planning tools
www.tutor2u.net/revision_notes_strategy.asp

Office of the Information Commissioner
www.dataprotection.gov.uk

Consumer law for competition and fair trading
www.tradingstandards.net
www.oft.gov.uk (Office of Fair Trading).

Office for national statistics
www.statistics.gov.uk

Change Management

Change management resource library
www.change-management.org/articles.htm

The change management section of this business portal is a useful
resource
www.business.com/directory/management/change_management/
reference/

Development for High Performance

American Society for Training and Development
www.astd.org/astd

Investors in People
www.investorsinpeople.co.uk

Chartered Institute of Personnel and Development
www.cipd.co.uk

Managing for Results

Motivation theories
www.accel-team.com/motivation/

ACAS – the UK arbitration site
www.acas.org.uk

Managing Yourself

Learning and learning styles from the guru, Peter Honey
www.peterhoney.com/product/brochure

Interesting articles about beliefs, emotions and positive thinking
www.personalpowernow.com.au/Articles/index.asp

Centre for Applied Emotional Intelligence
www.emotionalintelligence.co.uk/eitheory.htm

For Product Safety Concerns and Information please contact our EU
representative GPSR@taylorandfrancis.com Taylor & Francis Verlag GmbH,
Kaufingerstraße 24, 80331 München, Germany

Printed and bound by CPI Group (UK) Ltd, Croydon, CR0 4YY
01/05/2025
01858325-0001